O9-CFU-070

PITT POETRY SERIES

Ed Ochester, Editor

POET IN ANDALUCÍA

Andrea & Patrick

POET IN ANDALUCÍA

Nathalie Handal

UNIVERSITY OF PITTSBURGH PRESS

Published by the University of Pittsburgh Press, Pittsburgh, Pa., 15260
Copyright © 2012, Nathalie Handal
All rights reserved
Manufactured in the United States of America
Printed on acid-free paper
10 9 8 7 6 5 4 3 2 1
ISBN 13: 978-0-8229-6183-3
ISBN 10: 0-8229-6183-0

Contents

Preface

FEDERICO GARCÍA LORCA lived in Manhattan from 1929 to 1930, and the poetry he wrote about the city, *Poet in New York*, was posthumously published in 1940. Eighty years after Lorca's sojourn in America, and myself a poet in New York of Middle Eastern as well as Mediterranean roots, I went to Spain to write *Poet in Andalucía*. I recreated Lorca's journey in reverse.

Andalucía has always been the place where racial, ethnic, and religious forces converge and contend, where Islamic, Judaic, and Christian traditions remain a mirror of a past that is terrible and beautiful. *Poet in Andalucía* is a meditation on the past and the present. It renders in poetry a region that seems to hold the pulse of our earth, where all of our stories assemble. It is a meditation on what has changed and what insists on remaining the same, on the mysteries that trouble and intrigue us, and on a poet who continues to call us to question what makes us human.

Lorca left as part of his legacy a longing for homeland. My own longing stretches across four continents, due to a life made exilic by the political turmoil in the Middle East. His poems are about discovering a lost self. The poems in this collection confront that same loss and resonate with that same yearning for a sustaining place. *Poet in New York* is about "social injustice and dark love" and the quality of otherness such forces produce. *Poet in Andalucía* explores the persistent tragedy of otherness, but it also acknowledges a refusal to remain in that stark darkness and searches for the possibility of human coexistence.

Lorca arrived in New York in 1929 and moved to the dorms at Columbia University, where I have taught on and off for close to a decade. He spent Christmas that year *on the Hudson*. My journey in Spain started in December 2009, and I spent Christmas that year in Benalmádena, one of the hundred towns of Málaga province. Because I was based in Málaga, that's the province in Andalucía I lived in longest. I traveled widely throughout Andalucía: Córdoba; Sevilla, including Huelva and Cádiz (such as Arcos de la Frontera, Jerez de la Frontera, Tarifa and Algeciras) provinces; and of course, Granada and its surroundings, the Sierra Nevada, Las Alpujarras, Jaén and Almería provinces.

During Lorca's trip he also ventured outside of New York City. Outside of Andalucía, I went to Catalunya, namely, Barcelona, Figueres, L'Armentera, then exploring dozens of villages and towns in the area. I also spent time in Madrid, Castilla-La Mancha (Toledo being a highlight), and Galicia (staying a few months in the Santiago de Compostela). Finally, Lorca went to Havana; my Havana was Tangier.

When Lorca returned to Spain, he wrote feverishly and so did I. He gave readings of his poems and explained how they came into being. The audiences' reactions and his revelations during these exchanges guided him while he wrote *Poet in New York*. He explained how he immersed himself in the places he went to before delivering his lyrical reaction of them. He spent nine months in America, I finished a draft of *Poet in Andalucía* nine months after I arrived in Spain.

Andalucía is lyrical. Even if I had not consciously set to recreate Lorca's journey in reverse, I would have sought in my poems the region's songfulness.

And you, lovely Walt Whitman,stay asleep on the Hudson's banks
with your beard toward the pole, openhanded.

Federico García Lorca,
"Ode to Walt Whitman,"
Poet in New York

Everything stirs up the memory
of my passion for you
still intact in my chest
although my chest might seem
too narrow to contain it.

Ibn Zaydun, "Written from al-Zahra"

POET IN ANDALUCÍA

I

Poems of Soledad con Biznagas in Málaga

Para Alberto López

Ojalá

He holds on to the force
that stretches the narrow light
and finds himself somewhere behind history.

He thinks,
All we have left
is to invent God,
to find an infinite number to hope in,
to touch the grounds of La Manquita,
say *Insha'allah*,
and wait for the church bells
to remind us of who we have become.

He knows what it means
to live in another sleep —
time moving over faces.

There are different varieties of loss —
his is contemplating
water trapped in mouths,

his is never entering
La Malagueta,

his is trying
to understand
what *God willing* means,

or if that is what we say
to erase the fog on our tongue.

Walking to the Alcázar

Esta es la dulce Málaga, llamada de Bella, de donde
son las famosas pasas, las famosas mujeres y el vino
preferido para la consagración.

Rubén Darío

Who rewrites what's slanted,
the shape of the position you just left,
how your body molds the air,
leaving a fixed space?

I leave different shapes of me
all over Málaga—

I walk Alameda Principal
and people pass by me
as if they know something
I don't. Franco is gone,
but it's difficult to forget
the map of bones
he left behind.

The Puerto opens up,
waiting for a message or a breeze—
no one can hide anything from the sea,
people fill the chiringuitos,
and Rubén awaits at the end of the avenida.

Now facing the Gibralfaro
I accept the moment,
what will come.
I ask about the rampart, the Coracha, the Alcazaba,
ask about the limestones, the Patio de los Naranjos,
the gunpowder, and the Airón Well.

Where are you Rubén?
What haven't you shown me,
what do you look like undressed,
what do the earth and the waters
have in common
when a woman presses her breast against them?

My clothes are now wet,
it's winter,
I belong nowhere this minute,
it begins to rain.

My voice accepts the other voice—
Arabic then Spanish.
The ocean is broken
but not even that can divide us.

Nothing belongs to me,
but I am here and you exist—
you keep showing me
the way love moves what's past.

The Wounded Horse and a Tree in an Old Night

Village after village
I move
gather salt
some biznagas
what would the ruin say

It's not possible to flee
the past or the thunderstorm
death or the heart

A bird passes by unsure

Like the photo of a boy
with his father
in Basque Country 1937

The faces yellow
their names unknown

A bombing
gray black and white
a soldier with an open palm
a mother staring
at a light bulb
a human skull a bull
and a pale horse —
can peace rest
among bodies
unmoving

A shadow by a horn
waiting to find the open window
on the dark wall

On the dark wall an open window
Plaza de la Merced
where he was born—
how would he paint his birth
or his baptism
in la Iglesia de Santiago

I look at the church's Mudéjar tower
walk Calle Granada

and my breath aches
death is closer to life
than we accept
and we try counting—

they were killed early
they kissed early
they roamed the city early
they forgave the earth no more
nor did they forgive the ant bites
the sun's rays
and they were thankful
to those who wanted
to bring them back
by knowing
their age
name
face
by taking the thorn out
of their ashes

A bird passes by

A tree in an old night

See the wounded horse

And moves toward me
as I move toward a village

Like a ghost gathering
what the ruin said
except we weren't there to hear

Gypsy with a Song

I could take Harlem night and wrap around you.
Langston Hughes, "Juke Box Love Song"

I was born far from a plain
close to a church
far from a stream
close to a field
far from a God with eyes

Smoke curls like thick fog
a song
by Duke Ellington is playing—
trumpets teasing souls

I'm in St. George's Anglican cemetery
in Málaga
where musicians and lovers of jazz
gather to play tunes
by tombs

A gypsy
I've wandered the globe
especially the shadows
I've spent life without a song—
day after day drifting along
but tonight
my song is in every campfire
every violin
my song is here
along with some happiness
some version of peace
some feet tapping earth
and the ocean deciding time

This is how it begins—
I am in your arms now
where I belong
am not a gypsy
not gitana
without a song
sin una canción
no
not no more
no more
I carried the Mississippi
and the Dead Sea
black folks and brown folks
the delta
the delta
la voix de la Nouvelle Orléans
and that of Harlem
here with me

All here—
the stretching of time
against hills
the drummer
the Moors
the heart aging
down a valley

Tonight
I am not a gypsy
I wear water like song
its moistness
its hum
its banjo
its guitarra
and the whisper coming
like a cry abandoned some place

Canta
faster
faster
sing
until the Teatro de la Libertad
(Teatro Cervantes)

sing
until Atarazanas

until Antigua Casa de Guardia

until the tunes
cross
the river Guadalmedina

The color here —
is in the trombone
the cornet
in the hand that stops fire

Tonight I have a song —
about sharp wild breath
three windows
one echo
a slow shadow
that no longer pretends
it knows what it sees

Tonight I am a gypsy with a song
about belonging, and longing
the second set —
a drowsy tune
the speed of solitude

Tomás Heredia, 8

When I leave Tomás Heredia, 8
I imagine someone
will volunteer to walk past
the thought
evening is having,
and another will pretend
to look for answers,
but who wants to know
what it's like
to be oneself
all the time?

The prostitutes will stand waiting,
while others watch the city view
from the AC Málaga Hotel,
have a seco at the Larios Hotel
or churros con chocolate at Casa Aranda.

The man across the street
will finally repair the window
that holds sunlight
in the broken edges of the glass
where every hour I observed his face
and with no conclusion
as to why he insisted on sitting
by the only shattered window of his house.

I abandoned my post one afternoon
and spent time with the sounds
on the side streets instead,
and the wall by the kitchen,
now wet—
a huge stain darkening the yellow paint,

damaging the back of a painting
the owner,
Señor Isaac Jiménez Albéniz,
bought in Nerja.

When I leave Tomás Heredia, 8
the shadows will tell me
that they are not lines nor circles,
not movement, not sound,
but small gestures,
reflecting backward on the wall.

✓ Biznagas

To belong
even if you've kept the hours
in your closet—
it takes years

to forget a person
who merely looked up at you—
it takes years

to understand why
while you walk
the leaves dictate
how your heart
will beat—
it takes years

it takes years
to hold the wind
in your mouth
have it accommodate what it can't
a history
the clash of two moons
the slopes after heavy rain

and then the biznagas
remind you—
it takes years
to come back
from the direction
that divides you

I I

Maktoub, the Moor Said

She is an immigrant from other lands.
When she stretches out her ebony wings
shows her ivory body
opens her sandalwood beak
and laughs with great guffaws
it's a sign of good weather.

> *Ghalib ibn Ribah al-Hajjam,*
> *"The Stork," eleventh century, Toledo*

El País

The hills move an inch—
no sound by the tree
no whisper, no hour to speak of,
no dream
but a misplaced light
he should be aware of,
the word *fulano*
echoing inside of him.
Music migrates too.
He looks at the *El País*,
wonders
who is wise enough
to understand
when a country runs
toward a man
tells him,
we leave behind our life
for others to love,
leave, what sound can't destroy.

And he thinks,
will Machado return?

Tree of Red Leaves, Jaén 2009

I try to remember everything—
the clothes he wore in 1975,
black slacks, a white shirt, short sleeves.
I try to remember where he hid
his soul—under the book
he bought in Jaén, 1939,
under the gallery table made of echoes.
I try to remember when they opened his body
to check his temperature—107 degrees.
I try to remember when he felt lost
in his small corner—
a space too tiny for breathing.
When he had no memory with him—
his life without the bag of testaments,
without the number etched in his mind.
When he had no glass, no plate, no fork,
and used the same paper cup,
the same paper plate,
one small plastic fork,
until he had no choice but to surrender—
that's when he told me
A *tree of red leaves can break your heart.*
I try to remember him
without his mouth open,
without death hanging on his tongue.
I try to remember
what he told me, word for word
about the day he hid from the sun,
that there is a certain light
that brings war back.
But he was warned,
there is no such thing as perfect shade.

Paraguas Perdido

They come from Ecuador—
want another flag
want their universe
to be made
of European coins
and old reverie.

They want the origins of holy,
of water
in both hands,
a factory of metal
and tears.

A sun never goes for too long—
the rain
means more rain.
The acres of trees—all oranges—
are many,
the city close enough
to the beats of their pulse
they have been counting
since Ronda.

The sound of their reverie—
sleep that winds time,
a clock
refusing.

An architect, now a farmer,
measures distance
and the fine angles
that chart another *vega*.

A mouth moves
over a page of wings,
over an elegy
tipping,
a match unlit
and a direction
no one bothered to remember.

No teahouse, no light, no river,
keeps me for long here,
an Ecuadorian tells me,
like a lost umbrella—
at times wanted, often forgotten—
but I am thankful, for now,
the night has
left the rain elsewhere.

The Courtyard of Colegiata del Salvador ✓

We are strange when we're lost,
his father told him.
Saïd didn't hear the rest.
He couldn't count the waves
that led him across
the Strait of Gibraltar
so he tore his memory,
left where he came from behind,
and learned to pray differently.
He knelt instead of bowed.
He counted stones,
drew the church columns,
spoke any language but his own.
Years later, sitting
in a courtyard he is startled
by the loudness of the wind,
almost like the start of the *adhan*.
He feels a small fire
alongside his heart,
and hears his father's voice —
we are nothing
but an image
growing from our sleep —
how do we explain
our journey to others?
He looks at the grounds of the courtyard
where a mosque once stood
and understands what his father hadn't —
what's sacred always returns.

Sacromonte

They sing,
say that the blue hour
listening to flamenco
is when the world hides it's grief.
They love,
call the moon *el pasado*,
the mountain *el destino*.
They use
their roaming souls
to see water wishing.
They move
ivory in their daydreams.

I go to where they weep,
discover what their smiles say,
motion after motion —
I cross
each curve,
the road
winding,
the old pieces of the heart
scattered,
a new confusion,
and a dance.

Gitano. Gitano. Gitano.
The river here is alive,
the view too,
the white houses,
the caves,
the smell of tobacco,
the small wooden chairs,
and the castañuelas,

the music that slips through
the cracks of the ground
and gives you the silence of freedom,
a freedom like an eclipse,
owning the skies,
a love
made of water,
a ray
made of water,
and to your right
and to your left,
a blazing wind
destroying the sounds
of exile,
and the wanderings
the gitanos have crossed
and now,
the road, the side street, the dark corner,
is a version of home.

The Moor

This is what I see:

a grain of wheat in the hand of a small boy

barefoot on the unnamed roads,
sleeping in the dream another is having.

An oud, a violin, a guitar,
a mirror of dew,

a man about to undress,
a woman staring.

A traveler
returning
everywhere

and forgetfulness
stealing from itself.

Maktoub, the Moor says,
we hold clouds in our mouth
and imagine God in our breath.

I I I

Alleys and Reveries

Sólo una voz, a lo lejos,
siempre a lo lejos la oigo,
acompaña y hace ir
igual que el cuello a los hombros.

Miguel Hernández

Christmas in Benalmádena

What are we hiding
when we open someone else's door

Outside
the sea the sand the village
you and I and the mountain

Inside
laughter by a fireplace
a letter full of commas
a tray of turrón
and a guest telling another guest—
touch the door where your lover lived
touch the handle where you placed
your grief for the first time
touch the flame that meant
something to you

Isn't that what happens in celebration—
hearts move in windows?

On the Way to Jerez de la Frontera

Maybe you are missing
a part of you,
or you are out of questions,
or you are nowhere in sight
and everyone's looking for you.

Maybe noise
is where pleasure lives,
where a version
of death hides.

Maybe we know nothing
of what surrounds us,
and the sherry we drink—
fino, amontillado, oloroso—
fills us with what we can't desire
for too long.

We need to invent something
about ourselves:
the country we are from,
this striking white color,
this empty shadow,
and the paper burning
inside of it, inside of it
the distance
moving
ash in the back of our eyes.

The Thing about Feathers ✓

We kept only the keys,
letters, and photos—
everything else stayed behind
when we left the house.
That can happen when
a nation changes overnight,
when those you know
turn into
a gate of feathers—
and the thing about feathers is,
they know what's been missed.
For years I watch
my neighbor's house
from others' windows—
different countries,
various homes,
some of brick, some of stone.
Some never imagine
what a home can mean
when an unfinished tune
traps the ceiling.
I pretend
never to have
seen a body midair,
a father's hands
planted on the ground—
after all
what we don't admit to
never happened.
But I couldn't
change that day in Murcia,
when water brought light
to the door:

I am seven
it is the day before our departure,
the day my father
gives me a notebook,
and I tell him,
this is where I'll keep my country.

Now That

Ahora que está tan sola la soledad

Joaquín Sabina, "Ahora que"

Now that we've counted
the seasons for exile
and stopped wondering
if it's us or the birds who weep

Now that the canvas is wet
and paint drips on our bodies
now that we have crossed
the borders of hearts
and know what's real
now that disappearance
can't be understood after all

Now that we stay in bed
and I lay you out inside of me
now that streets are empty
and you press a compass to your chest
stack a sorrow after a wound
and measure the map of want

Now that two people run inside of you
one searching for its lost head
while the other watches
now that we have learned
to love each other
the way we are told we should

Now that I say goodbye
and write about leaving
I feel alive
now that nothing is urgent

and everything is here
now that waiting keeps us away
from a forest of thorns

Prophet in Andalucía ✓

We love in the morning,
close our eyes to forget it's early.
We name the street
with a drawing of a hundred
Jesuses on the wall.
We try to define beauty,
what tells us that we should have kept
our eyes open when we could.
We hear voices against the wind,
look at the sea,
discover what's broken,
invent the rules of drowning.
We ask ourselves if
the white villages are absent
when we long,
if we are phantoms
dreaming ourselves as flesh,
if the prophet
is buried in the mind's unbearable song.

IV

Constelación en el Ateneo de Sevilla

Light passing through wine
reflects on the fingers
of the cupbearer
dyeing them red
as juniper stains
the muzzle of the antelope.

Abu l-Hasan Ali ibn Hisn,
"Reflection of Wine,"
eleventh century, Sevilla

Los pájaros la saludan,
porque piensan (y es así),
que el Sol que sale en Oriente
vuelve otra vez a salir
en la verde orilla
de Guadalquivir.

Luis de Góngora y Argote

Seven Stars in Sevilla

December '27

1. Rafael Alberti

¿Adónde el Paraíso, sombra, tú que has estado?
Pregunta con silencio.

You rest your voice on the white roofs.
I rest my eyes on the ports where I saw
my grandmother once. She thought
it was Tripoli. We are in Cádiz.
You stand at the bottom of the night
with the rain. I stand under the lightning
not too far away. You dismantle summer
to find your feet. I take the day apart
to find a compass. You tell me
we must accept the sun now.
So I stay behind. I keep the heat.
You pass the streets, the cars, the women,
you even pass your heart.
The sailors prepare to float away,
and you ask them to describe water,
look at the roofs,
and the time you touched
the tears on your face
and kept them from falling—
the ground wants everything.
That was then. Now, there is only
one sentence in your head—
where is that place?

2. Gerardo Diego

Habrá un silencio verde, todo hecho de guitarras destrenzadas.
La guitarra es un pozo con viento en vez de agua.

Early afternoon. You try to understand
the small steps silence takes
to find a certain order.
That's what you wanted.
Not a guitar. Not a song. Not a voice.
Not a gunshot passing through the window.
You wanted to fold love over the heart,
hold silence so that it doesn't grow.

3. Juan Chabás

No, amor, nadie lo sabe; nadie, ni tú, mi amor,
sabe que estoy esperando contigo . . .

I put my shoes on
while his shoe was still in the water—
a stream separated our thoughts,
a ray of sunlight
under his chin.
What I knew then
I still believed later on:
We collected the same flames,
but our breath grew short too fast,
and nothing can really happen twice,
not the same smile, the same kiss
and we should know by now,
when we wait, that something haunts us—
no one can describe love
precisely.

4. Dámaso Alonso

Cuando yo te maté, mirabas hacia fuera, a mi jardín.
Este diciembre claro me empuja los colores y la luz.

A mask
in the center of a circle

A hill
swelling the mind

Here water is made
of bone and muscle

Here a mirror
is where leaves change colors

Where nothing happens happens
where voices grow rain

Where air is a translucent glow
above our heads

Where butterflies land
by the small moons along the coast

Here we meet—who says
the dead are incapable of humor

¿El mundo cabe en un olvido?

There is ecstasy when breath meets breath,
when the space between opponents
looks at the forest in the sky,
when cold water becomes dream—
a passing through
meadow after meadow after meadow.
There is no solitude. No exile.
No cosmos around your ankles,
just a pain hesitating around your bones,
a few decades old.
The coffins have long emptied out the hearts—
that's where the young are.
A labyrinth collides with itself.
Who said we can leave
something so splendid—
that's what we are told about war.
Where is the ocean,
where has the sand gone—
is this July air lifting the breeze to music?
Hurry, there is a horse trying to pass by,
a dew trying to move the city away,
a displaced fog trying to gather
the pieces of freedom.
We invent our forgetting,
but still hear
the voice trapped in the back of the closet—
in the corner, the sun stays low.

6. José Bergamín

No tengo más realidad que la irrealidad del tiempo.

This last drum. This last train.
This last hour. Last warning.
This is history.
A thousand feet pacing a country,
voices ripping up the winter sky,
an obsession at the edge of a world
and there, a decision —
you either believe in it or you don't.
That's the trouble with time —
the only way out of it is in.

7. Federico García Lorca

Deja tu corazón en paz, Soledad Montoya.

The walls are thinner now,
my hands hold on to the noise you left,
the loss deafening the room.
Look, there is fire under the Persian rug,
there is a line of silver glowing
around your cigarette.
Give me a lily,
tell me the story about the moon,
when it moved our bodies
to make a place for the dove
in the back of our hearts.

V

In Córdoba

And although it was still night,
when you came, a rainbow
gleamed on the horizon,
showing as many colors
as a peacock's tail.

Ibn Hazm (994–1063),
"My Beloved Comes," Córdoba

Alhandal y las Murallas de Córdoba

The ocean is hanging
by the garden of la Mezquita,
and the roof is covered with birds—
white, a few gray—
its red and white stripes
revealing what it's like to pray here.

People will build together again,
you tell me quietly,
as if no one is meant to hear.
Then you ask, where are
the cities of our childhoods,
and those of our deaths—
who will you be?

I tell you—
I will be
the hilltop
and the ground that split open
to allow the jasmines to bloom.

I will be
the jade
the bone collector sold
to see the woman he loves.

I will be
the well where water meets water.

I will invent my own languages,
images,
streets and sins,
my own walls and my own cities.

I will be
the two doors in the fading light,
the echo that burns his lips,
and the canvas that keeps the cry wet.

I will be
a house of dreamers,
a red garden,
an address,
and the woman who
memorized what
no one ever read.

Where is that home—
does it have something to do with my name?

I said my name but couldn't hear it,
said it again but the pronunciation was off,
said it one more time,
then heard someone else saying it correctly.

I couldn't say my name
the way it was meant to be said
and then I thought—
there is too much smoke in my lungs,
and I can't find the plaque that says Handal Stairs—
maybe I am in the wrong place,
or died, and morning never came.

The last time I said my name
you asked me to write a poem instead—
there are things no one can take away,
like flame covering feet with sand,
like the taste of date after a declaration,
like the walls of Córdoba —
a poem about tolerance.

I count the notes you left
on my tongue,
count the lamps
from Galicia,
Extremadura, Víznar,
the poems by Ibn Zaydun and Ibn Hazm,
Góngora and Quevedo,
and know there is an ancient path,
a door frame,
a prayer.

This is it,
water
receding
to make a place for mourners.

This is it,
cliffs moving to
find the sun,
love
moving
toward those who borrow
arrows for living.

But where is the match
to quiet death?

Where is Córdoba,
where I am?

I waited for you
where space breaks fire
into small planets.

Which prophet is yours,
and who will be judged?

I contemplate my return
to my name,
its origin,
exact location,
exact handwriting,
exact curves,
its valleys,
yellow rolling field,
its infinite green.

Stones are layered
like pearl necklaces
but I am lost
on a road I know—
has it changed or have I?
Has the land moved?

I see a jug of water,
a woman looking at her
reflection—
the past is what we are
looking for.

The past is here,
the song of the Arabs here,
the song of the Jews,
the Romans,
the Spaniards,
and the phantoms.

I find myself elsewhere,
especially everywhere here,
but mostly in the ruins.
I see myself in the stranger's face,
I hear my voice in hers—

what language am I speaking,
what am I wishing for,
am I entering or exiting
prayer or the alphabet?

I dream what I must.
The day you
told me,
Here is a bitter apple—
that's the meaning of your name—
it will help you find the days
that taught you who you are.

And I found
the day
my father gave me
a small bottle of blessed water.

The day Mary, Jesus, and Moses
wept together.

The day
I watched
three boys from Zahara de la Sierra
steal from the wind
and sing around the solitary watchtower
dominating the cliff where
Fatima is everywhere—
her five fingers
the five laws
of the Koran.

The day I wrote a poem
and Ibn Faraj, Ibn Iyad, and Ibn Sharaf
read it back to me.

The day
I saw
two men digging a hole
to bury those they'd betrayed.

The day
I knew there wasn't a nation
smaller than its dream.

The day I tried to move the sun
to find your shadow
under a rock.

See Córdoba, as I have—
enter Bab al-Yawz, now Almodóvar Gate,
it will lead you to the Judería,
the narrow squares, the ancient walls, the alleyways,
where you will meet Maimónides and Judá-Levi,
find Casa de Sefarad, the Sinagoga,
and square after square after square—
Corredera Square, Capuchinos Square.
When you reach Plaza del Potro,
have a drink with Don Quijote,
when you reach Plaza del Bailio,
look at the Hills of Bailio—
the view of Upper Medina and Axarquía,
and when you reach
the Alcázar de los Reyes Cristianos
pray east,

then walk to the Torre de la Calhorra,
stop at los baños árabes,
at a tetería
then a courtyard
where you will find
bitter apples scattered everywhere

and one bag of mesbahas
to take us to the place we left peace.

~

On a small stone
I find the note
about the evening
you, I, and
a small wind in autumn
deceived someone, or was it
declared something,
a dove on the mountain,
on the horns,
on the eagle,
on the anthem,
on *la vega*.
I have inherited your shadows
and a thousands crossroads.

You sigh — the stream is but an image.
Sigh — the mocking just a stranger without humor.
Sigh again — then start guessing
where I might have hidden
the Old Testament,
the New Testament
and the first version of
Don Quijote de la Mancha,
and what I found in Oviedo?

I wonder who waits for us
and who will disappear first
when they see Córdoba.

I feel close to death tonight.
I just saw the poets
of the Golden Ages and those of '27,

there was no time between them—
Luis told me *drink Natalya*,
Rafael told me *recite a Sura*,
Garcilaso told me *illusion creates history*,
Federico told me *sing to us*,
But it's what Lope told me that I remember most,
who declares love on whom
when doves cover the broken fences.

I took Lope's words and looked for
sea lavenders, crown daisies, wild gladiolus,
gray-leaved cistuses, and bishop's weeds,
to give to those who mourn,
those about to wed,
and especially those waiting
in lines
for miracles,
wheat field after wheat field.

I ask myself
where it all went—
what we hoped,
what we harvested,
what happened to those
who taught us winter's secrets
here or there,
gazelle after gazelle,
wheat field after wheat field.

I ask
What is precise after all—
not the trees,
not shadowlands,
not Isabel,
or the army,
not what hunts late
or early,

not what defends houses,
not living not even dying.

So stand—
look at Córdoba,
allow it to be what it is,
glorious and alive.

But perhaps
nothing is nothing—
change exists at every port,
every tree,
after every glass of Rioja.

Now is gone,
gone—
the unbearable weight of heat
in our memory,
the echo we carried
caravan after caravan—
and here we are
by la Mezquita
finally,
and the gate is gone,
the wind not wind,
the door
just a frame
holding a note—
but what's the use
of reading it now,
the heart beating so faintly?
Now is gone
but I still look at you as if
forgetfulness has taken its time.

We are bare—
without flag and music,

without guards and rulers,
without singers and poets,
without guitars and ouds.
Now is gone
and the sea too
and the sinners.
Now is gone
but not the wall of Córdoba,
the poems of Sufis,
or the Spanish language,
not Andalucía
its pomegranates, almonds,
oranges and oranges,
its ancient walls
and its heart,
shoulders, tongue,
back, arms, hand,
its shiver
all along absence.

Deep in your eyes,
that's where the trick is,
don't you see,
petals grow petals,
leaves bend to the wind
to accept their sentence—
a white deer passes—
and the myth, the wings, the tribes,
the saints, and the gloom
disappear in the drawings
on the walls.
I see Unamuno
and his shadow on the wall
facing east,
I see a boy listening to cante grande
then a *zajal* by the wall
facing south,

and in the middle,
I see the orange tree
that draws its shape on the ground,
that gives a wing to a traveler,
gives a simile to a poet,
gives a memory to a shepherd,
gives an image of a beautiful woman to a withered world,
gives the map of a labyrinth to a wanderer,
and breaks into sound.
Who says we can be free?
Everything we hear
is the echo of a voice we can't hear,
everything we see
the reflection of something we can't see.
The heart like a star
gives light to the color blue,
to the ruins of Córdoba.
And by la Mezquita,
by the walls
I give you alhandal —
to save you —
and you say my name for me.

10 Qit'as

Acitara

Can the sky recover after a bombing,
can a house break into two cities,
and secrets hold the wall
between two bodies?
Tell me, what are borders?

acitara: wall, from the Arabic *sitarah*, which means curtain.

~

Alfanje

History is nothing more
than the smell of dew in our bones
but even dew hurts
when it enters the heart,
even dragonflies know
what's unholy,
even a child scatters his hurt
to keep what's dead
alive in the mirror—
yes, somewhere
another crime is being committed.

alfanje: backsword with curved blade, from Arabic *al-khinjar*,
which means dagger.

~

Ajimez

We hesitated to
see the bent,
maybe we divided
our windows
to have a clearer view,
we gave birth
in languages not our own,
we wanted to hang
their photos
but
there were
no walls.

ajimez: mullioned window, from Arabic *samis*, one of the
distinctive features of Islamic buildings in Spain, especially
noticeable on minarets.

~

Ajaraca

Every loop a memory:
a field of lavender mist,
an ebony door,
an attic of white marbles,
wearing identical shoes,
suddenly, a house comes back.

ajaraca: ornamental loop in Andalusian and Arabic architecture,
from Andalusi Arabic *ash-sharakah*.

~

Zaga

Don't be distracted
by the young boy
you once were—
look,
something is moving
in the opposite direction.

zaga: rear, from Arabic *saqah*.

~

Aduar

If shadows crowd
only one side of the road,
they say, the street is broken
and death
can't cross
a broken street.

aduar: Bedouin or Gypsy settlement, from Arabic *duwwar*.

~

Adafina

He said:
A heart that contains ash
contains only ash.

adafina: stew that Spanish Jews used to place on glowing embers
on Friday evening to eat on the Sabbath, from Arabic *dafina*,
which means buried or covered.

~

Ahorría

When we hesitate
salt rises from the water

ahorría: barrenness or freedom, from Arabic *al-hurriya*.

~

Noria

It's better to drown
than to miss water —
confessions can't handle thirst.

noria: waterwheel or Ferris wheel, from Arabic *na'urah*.

~

Alafia

The doors are shut now —
the ghosts sit upright.

alafia: pardon or mercy, from Andalusi Arabic *al afya*, from
classical Arabic *afiyah*, health.

Patios

1

A long-awaited rain.
I know the name of nothing.
I have no words for what hurts.
I know that the trees around me
can answer what man can't—
something to do with love unmapping.
Assaqifa, someone tells me in Arabic.
Here, I respond,
we have a common language for patio.

2

It was our year, and then it was 1936.
I was imprisoned. She escaped.
I saw her two times after that.
She sent me letters and photos.
It's been fifty years now.
I'm writing her from the same cell—
her child about to get married.
Nothing about accepting this is human.
I'd like to say I feel distant,
but her lips are closer now,
for that's what happens with time;
you collect stories,
but you are in none of them,
except that afternoon in Córdoba—
red, pink, and yellow flowers circling us,
windows on lips.

3

She is standing by the geraniums.
Past eleven. Past the small fountain.
She is wearing a green dress.
She asks me if I've seen him.
I hesitate, then remind her he's died.
She leans over and kisses my forehead.
I forgot to tell him she was coming.

VI

By the Door, or Is It Death

Sparks shooting from his eyes
and wearing a poppy on his head
he arises to announce the death of night.

Al-As'ad Ibrahim ibn Billilah,
"The Rooster," eleventh century,
Toledo

Dado

He longs for
the secret forms of god
stretched
along the back of his neck

He longs for
what whispers
are stealing
by the slanted door

He asks
what the vision of a lotus is
against flesh
if not a trick

He longs for
the hallucinations numbers have
and the latitude of
an echo against an echo

He longs for
what can't die — evidence
that wild irises
can turn smoke into a republic

La Guerra

The newspaper stained our hands,
as if holding on to paper
would prevent our fall.

You said:
After the bomb,
I held a comrade's arm,
listened to Radiocadena Española,
and looked at the moon.
The bodies weren't moving.
I went closer—
we must remember
what we looked like once,
a country cut in half.

And there she was,
lying by the sidewalk
still faithful to what she believed,
her body stiff,
her hands open,
as if she knew I'd find her—
it was her way of giving me
another chance to change sides,
or it was my chance to take her with me—
that's all I wanted—
but she wouldn't let me do
even that,
the smile on her face
louder than my pleading—
this was not the nation we dreamed.

So I walked away,
tried to remember

what her heart looked like
when it was not outside her chest,
when she kissed me for the first time
and thought
I was on her side.

While Waiting for Death

When I die
a map of the world will
hang over my bed,
the small library in Mijas
where I read Lorca
for the first time
will become a café,
the olive trees
I can't live without
will be in full blossom,
I will see death from a distance
waiting for me
but I will not move—
I will die on a train
where the view will be
of white trees suspended
on gray clouds,
I will die in the sky
where birds will
carry a steam of light
on their wings,
I will die in a car
where the windows
will be a quilt of snow,
I will die moving.

As I wait,
my lover will say *you're beautiful*.
He will mean, I miss the sea.

I will say,
I don't know the word for life,

but know we must play
so that it's not only about death.

He will ask,
why do we grow stillness—
is it a noise we are close to,
where the stones and flies and trees and birds
and echo and earth and what hides
behind them insists on music?

A song will swipe by us.

I will look at him, he too will be waiting—
but I am not certain for what exactly.

Then I will think, solitude knows
it's where the empty space is,
and death knows it shouldn't count
while it waits.

VII

Granada

The wine is the rising sun,
her mouth the setting sun,
the hand of the assiduous
cupbearer, the east.

> *The Umayyad Prince Marwan ibn*
> *'Abd al-Rahman (d. 1009),*
> *"The Beauty at the Revels,"*
> *Central Andalucía*

✓ Sheets of Dry Wind

We drift above the plain,
the gold sky, the pines, the chopos,
the voice of old flamenco,
there are no barbed wires here,
no unusable vessels of stars.
There is a fainting arm
that says it all —
something about a heart,
the way it holds the garden close,
like holding on to a temptation,
like Christ being near.

When will water part,
when will the sea sing hunched,
the winter break into raindrops?

Why do we speak of pain?
Perhaps we are thirsty,
perhaps Galilee is *la vega*,
and all the olive groves have moved
to Andalucía —
a mouth over another mouth,
a way of saying
this is what's untouchable,
sheets of dry wind.
You see,
it's what's inside of us
that holds the pieces
we can't reach.

Granada Sings Whitman

By the river Genil
lovers sing what belong to the water,
a shoemaker sings the dream he had,
his helper the dream he didn't,
a man sings to the woman
on the broken mattress,
death at midday sings,
on the banks of the Darro
a blind thief
collecting golden poplars sings,
and so does the crevice of quivers,
the saints flaming in la Sierra
and the men rehearsing a country.
They know nothing stays,
but when Whitman sings—
they allow his voice
to take them apart.

VIII

Convivencia

Stop beside Honey River
stop and ask

> *Ibn Abi Rawh, "Honey River,"*
> *twelfth century, Algeciras*

Awon / Sin

We will tell each other that
we can't choose
between one country and another,
we will tell each other
that we will kill
even if we don't want to,
we will regret saying it
and we will start
all over again.
Your pain will hang inside mine,
mine inside yours, you will
comb my hair, and I will comb yours.
You will press your ears against my wall,
I will press mine against your body,
we will love and search
we will try and live
with what follows us—
but no one can change this:
we are unable to tear
our eyes from each other.

Convivencia / Two Ghazals Two Tzvis

Ghazal / 1

Sometimes music presses its ache against the mirrors
so that a thousand windows can find a heart.

On the terrace of wild jasmines, we see a sky cut into pieces,
and we bow to keep the small clouds in the heart.

The fog hides one hundred violins in the groves of our childhood,
but under the palm tree, our breath continues to grow the heart.

In the withering garden of daybreak, we starve to translate grief,
at the end of a well, ghosts sculpt water into hearts.

Night comes so that you can come so that the wet jasmines can
    stay wet
and the voice can bend to listen to the soft wave at the bottom of
    the cup.

Tzvi / 1

The light covers the stairs
she sees her reflection

on the wet floor
she sees his

they stare at each other
and their shadows tell them

get out fast, leave, forget
this is forbidden

and then a bucket of water
washes their faces from the tiles

he sees her nipples under her shirt
and she the ripples of water

moving over his feet—
a country never ends.

Ghazal / 2

Under the secret part of desire, an albérchigo—
It's there I see the opening of a scarf of concerto

He starts with cero
and ends with solo

I saw his face once, he stood inside, outside an algarazo,
now diwans are piled up in front of the window to keep his
    last echo

On the balcony, one forgotten azulejo—
when I look closer, I see our faces trapped, yes, it's that photo

At the dark corner of the zoco
we hide letters in the back of a radio

Tzvi / 2

Eight hundred years of love—
we can't be strangers now.

We are here to allow
the other to be here.

There is a sea beyond the sea.
But who is watching us when we make love?

If your heart is not mine,
the kiss you placed on my neck is mine,

the word you drew on the palm of my hand is mine,
your touch, that afternoon on the banks, is mine,

the continent you placed by the chariot is mine,
but what about this paradise, who is it for?

We knew we were both in it. We also knew,
we can't lose a paradise we've seen.

Abásho

Tell me what I should do
so when I awake
I see only the strands of your hair.
Tell me what I should do
so the songs don't break
the cellar in the room.
Tell me what I should do
to keep silence out of our way.
Tell me what I should do
to keep the sun out of your coat,
to find a way to obey the wind
to find the pomegranate on
the other side of the revolution.
There is a moth, there is a flame too—
desire is just another illusion.
Tell me, below—
is there a cathedral in the sea?
I turn on the only straight street
in my body and discover,
when we depart, a confession
rises in the bottom drawer.

The Book of Toledo

One night by the sea
a breeze was held against its will
in the morning the sea turned to black waters
(These words were inscribed on a wooden
bench by the Río Tajo)

The old fire
needs any excuse to start
igniting the ships
(These were the words of a sailor who witnessed
the war between the sea and a dictator)

You don't realize I am the ocean—
every time you shoot me
your bullet becomes a small island
for me to rest on
(These were the words a victim
dedicated to his enemy)

One soldier asks another,
How do you sleep
when you've killed so many?
Because when I shut my eyes
my dreams vanish
(This was a conversation on the Alcántara Bridge
between two deserters of a religious war)

When a wind is a guest in your house
make sure the windows are open
so it doesn't take everyone with it
(This was what one exile told another
by the Sinagoga del Tránsito)

In between the hanging ropes
my reflection—one I could see
only when I stood far away—
when we leave home
we never stop looking for
images of the land on our faces
(These words were written on a wall
by the Mezquita del Cristo de la Luz)

Is that my mother's scarf
or a sparrow flying by
(These were the words of a peacemaker's son, eight,
a few seconds before he went blind and mute)

When a poet loses his mind
he goes to his words
when words can't bear
their meaning
they go to prayer
when prayer
can't see the black mountain
it turns to God
(These are the words of a man
without a country)

They gave us blankets
a sky of a thousand faces
an ocean to swim
and instead of turning away,
we got lost in it
(These were the words of an immigrant
whose life was too short)

When will you come back to La Mancha
(This is my father's daily prayer)

IX

Flight to Catalunya and Afternoons in Galicia

A mi madre

Errantes, fugitivas, misteriosas,
tienden las nubes presuroso el vuelo . . .

Rosalía de Castro

Testament in Barcelona

History can't be rushed.
We didn't have time to see the village,
we didn't have time to see the house fall
to build light out of mud,
nor did we see time burning.
The city is missing,
and we've saved others,
our backs turned.
What happened
is a different reality in everyone's mind,
but the direction we took
tells us the world doesn't end
when we force air out of bones.
Now we know the myth
by the cup of coffee going cold,
realize we were never told
how to take
the street parallel to our heart.

Quartet in Catalunya

Ara
Something turns language into air in her musing
that's what missing is about, she thinks—when the town she
    is from
is wrapped in a white quilt woven by snow
and she's lost her way to La Rambla

Ara
She changes into a vintage dress,
she knows shadows stain death, that her lover is a black pine,
she knows the sounds love makes when she can't see
La Sagrada Familia from her window

Ara
She can't leave a room that fills the dark with something darker
so she flirts with things on the other side
and thinks of the circumference—
why the man she loves doesn't die

Ara
Noise breaks into sequence
Tibidabo moves the highest hill in her eyes
and forces her to see the city and ask herself
which temptation she worships

Waltz of a Dream

There is a dream of dance
that we'll remember
there's ten windows
where shoulders lean on
there is a piece of sun
ten echoes roaming
where love lost
is a place that becomes

Dance yes come dance

There's a chair
where death sits
there's a mirror
there's a garden
that cuts hell into hills

There's a shadow
that runs through the mirror
and a window that opens
the world

Dance yes come dance

There's a rooftop
where noise keeps its hat
where white ribbon and a cry
starts to fly
there are footsteps
that want all their shadows
there are lovers that want
all the waltz

Dance yes come dance

There's a hum
on your forehead that hums
this dream this dream this dream
yes this dream yes this dance

Santiago

He might return and if he appears blue I might
allow him on top and if he returns with the sun
I will let summer multiply on my body
and if he returns for the phrases in Galego
I will make him say them in Arabic

What we like most is what doesn't belong to us
like the field of stars and the Holy Door
like the coins lost on rooftops and the letters in Celtic
like the seascapes the wide rivers wild coastlines

If he returns I will write: Distance dreamed time
into lovers not into houses but a cosmos

Didn't I ever tell him he is most beautiful
when the arcaded stone streets inside him are wet
when I see him below Christ's feet and below him
Hercules, holding open the mouth of two lions?
I draw his body on the carpet
to stain what history gave to him

What can postpone departure beside two lips
too much of the wrong heart on the wrong road?
Hurry Rúa da Raiña into glory light into lush whispers
hurry the Atlantic into harmony the chaos into blaze
hurry the fisherman into piers the verse into our bedroom
then ask me to undress the rain
to go by the chimney barefoot
to caress my breast and count in your language
Santiago, let your lips draw the borders around mine

To Yolanda for opening Galicia to me

X

The Poet Arrives in Tangier and Afterward

A Nagib

Tanger Bleu

He gave her a *bakhshish*
and left—
it was too early for confusion.
He collected odd meanings
in the medina,
she collected laughter,
he wanted more of childhood,
she wanted more of the sea,
they needed more than their bodies
to confront themselves—
a flame in a leaf
a cool wind
a fez flying away.

She knew a journey
was like walking on the ocean,
like a prophet hiding glories,
but this was Tangier
and it was important to stay lost,
so the city took him from
one blank wall to another
to keep him asking for more.

He still came
to the Café Central every day,
still waited for her to say *Monsieur,*
still needed the mess of images,
the badly paved roads.
He liked that
there were hours
waiting by the sea,
there was a sun,

there was a crush
on the ground;
that air had broken
the window,
broken the small hums
and that version
of their heart.

He didn't know
how to imagine this—
he knew he didn't
owe death anything,
but he owed love;
he knew magic
accepted something
strange here,
but he didn't know
where the spirit was,
he knew that here
you get what you want
even if you don't know
what your want is.

He looked
at the *djellaba* by the chair,
the *kif* on the small wooden table,
the book by Mohamed Chouki—
what music do we record
when we record?
(What would she say?)
Like the drum the drum the drum,
the ruins and the cliffs,
like the first time he heard
Allah Akhbar
and slept in the desert—
there is no coming back
from solitude.

Then he was back.
C'est chaud, she said,
placed a small blue glass
in front of him
and whispered:
nostalgia is just something to do here,
there is also walking in the mud,
drinking tea,
and reading Tennessee Williams—
tell me,
how many
compassions does it take
before freedom
turns noise into an album.

He looked at her—
didn't she know
the ocean had missing pages,
that we had forsaken memory
and the sky
to deliver belief to a savior.
They say a man who looks
at the sea
knows
something about his soul,
though it's uncertain if salt
is heavy on the tongue,
if heroes wear masks,
and if when a man finally
understands grief—
which means he finally
understands history—
that's when
he knows how a face rots.
Quel bled, he finally answered.

They looked at each other
as the birds folded their wings,

like desire
bowing to something
they felt
but would never describe.

Yes, cities can't grow quiet
and neither can an empire:
they keep growing differently,
the television on again,
the flags rising—
who loves a nation best?
They tried to play the *qsbah*,
tried to remember the day
they promised
never to hurt each other,
but that was when
they still had sharp teeth.

Now they take each other apart
and look at a picture of
a city and a man waiting
for the same woman.

La Movida

He saw nothing. Said nothing.
He could no longer sleep in the room.
There are many ways to love —
What would you like me to see, I ask him?

I can't see you any longer.
I see you in every window,
and we hear the same thing,
now that I'm weeping
and you're kissing.

I wonder what lasts longer,
your lips on hers
or my kiss now further away.
That's the thing about freedom
it bends you over.
Do we need Almodóvar?

Are you watching
one of his films
without me?
Does Madrid miss me?

You envy me.
I know.
Open your eyes,
come closer,
I am alive in the light
and in your distance,
and something else.
I'm thinking about November —

will you be there,
or are you waiting for Pedro,
the chaos
an afternoon can bring?

The Traveler

If now your dream is at last aligned with your truth,
don't think this truth is any more fragile than the dream.

Luis Cernuda, "El Viajero"

Traveler, your footprints are the only road, nothing else
Traveler there is no road, only a ship's wake on the sea.

Antonio Machado, There is No Road, *XXIX*

Beneath a nomad, another
that's the way to guide whispers.
Making love lets us forget
the music limping around our feet,
reminds us
there is no precision in traveling—
it unweaves the body,
invents its lines and directions.
There is no precision—
except in knowing
the sea holds our waist
when we think we've gathered
what the skies have hidden
and what the road couldn't.

On My Way to Tamarit

On my way to Tamarit
I tell you *no puedo verte*

But I see
what drowns in the hearts of men
what exists at once on lips

On my way to Tamarit
you hide your face behind the moon
hide behind the route of doves
la astati'u an araka

But I see
the split rooftops
where will the birds land now
what can the Lord be that he doesn't know

At the train station
the morning asks too many questions
the body loses its map
demands new borders
as if we get anything
when we ask politely

On my way to Tamarit
I take my clothes off
wait for what comes next
la astati'u an araka

It is too late
it seems it's still too late
to love without patience
that's what keeps us loving

There is a chapel to the right
another to the left
no puedo verte

There is a line of people
waiting to confess
no puedo verte

There is a someone
crossing a line
that is what doubt does

That's how love breathes in us
like a country opening up finally

That's also how death arrives
not exactly on time but close enough

That's when my face turns on your shoulder
and you turn visible in the stains
on the streets on the walls
on the houses in the fields

I invented what was necessary
drew water on the back of the earth
and stopped measuring the silence
from your lips to mine
now we must unfold the pleats on our clothes
wounds only open to other wounds

No puedo verte
but on my way to Tamarit
I knew we didn't need to see
to give ourselves

Notes and Memories

¿De qué hablamos cuando hablamos solos?

Olvido García Valdés

From New York City to Andalucía

ON MY WAY to the airport, I think of the first time I went to Andalucía. It was 1988. I was eighteen years old. Twenty-one years ago. It's now December 22, 2009, also the twenty-fifth anniversary of the death of my paternal grandfather.

What I remember of that first trip was ritzy Marbella and my father running after a thief who had stolen a foreign woman's purse. He managed to grab the back of the thief's shirt and, being a robust man, pulled the thief toward him, grabbed the purse from his hand, and let him go. Everyone was so shocked that there was a long pause before the cheering started. My father always says we have to fight for what's *fair* and he religiously lives by that word.

I also remember walking with my parents in Mijas. There was something special about the town or the moment, as if we were returning to a memory. The white village on a hill, with its small old women dressed in black, is an image I've kept along the years. Later that same day, we went to eat at a tiny restaurant somewhere in la Costa del Sol. It was packed with people eating, drinking, and watching a fútbol match. My father laughed so much that afternoon I can still vividly feel his joy, hear it. It's one of the happiest moments I've ever seen in him.

Finally, Granada was what marked me most of all. We drove up the mountain; the olive trees were breathtaking, and the light against them added to their glory. It felt like home. That summer I read Lorca for the first time. I later discovered that in 1916, while at the University of Granada, Lorca went on a trip to Baeza with a few companions and his professor, Martín Domínguez Berrueta. Then eighteen years old, he met Antonio Machado, who introduced him to the work of Rubén Darío. Lorca, and eventually Machado and Darío, were to influence me later on during my undergraduate studies in Boston. My professor and now friend David Gullette and I engaged in numerous exchanges about these authors. I eventually wrote my thesis on Lorca.

Despite knowing David for more than two decades, I would meet his son, Sean, for the first time only while in Morocco during this most recent trip. He married the Moroccan artist Yto Barrada and lives in Tangier.

The well-known Arabist Emilio García Gómez went to Cairo in 1928. (In 1932, he became head of Granada's School of Arab Studies, established by the government.) There he discovered the unedited and unpublished codex of Ibn Sa'id (1243) entitled, *Rayat al-Mubarrizin wa-ghayat al mumayyzin*, translated as *The Banners of the Champions and the Standards of the Select Ones*. He published some of his prose translations of the poems in the *Revista de Occidente* in 1928, and those prose versions of the poems along with others later appeared in the collection *Poemas Arábigo-andaluces*. García Gómez wanted readers to have an idea of what Arab Andalusian poetry was like from the tenth to the thirteenth centuries. Unexpectedly, this collection was to influence the Generation of '27 and Lorca in particular. Rafael Alberti said in an interview that without García Gómez's translation Lorca's *El Diván del Tamarit* and other poems wouldn't have been possible. He also added that Arab and Jewish writers born in Spain "link up perfectly with our poets of the Golden Age . . . there is a continuity with the later poetry of Góngora, Soto de Rojas and centuries later, with our own." I first read those words in *Poems of Arab Andalusia*, translated by Cola Franzen (San Francisco: City Lights Books, 1989). I discovered these poems in 1989, and it took me more than twenty years to really go back to them. While writing this book, I reread the inscription written to me by their translator: "To Nathalie, May our first encounter be one of many to come!" Although Franzen and I never met again, while writing this book, these poems became my guide. The quotes by Arab Andalusian poets that introduce the sections in this book come from *Poems of Arab Andalusia*.

~

Preface

Richard L. Predmore writes that *Poet in New York* is about "social injustice, dark love and lost faith," in *Lorca's New York Poetry: Social Injustice, Dark Love, and Lost Faith* (Durham: Duke University Press, 1980).

Ian Gibson's *Federico García Lorca: A Life* (New York: Pantheon, 1989), was an important reference during this journey.

Olvido García Valdés is an award-winning poet and writer, born in 1950 in Santianes de Pravia, Asturias. She won the Premio Nacional de Poesía 2007 for her book, *Y todos estábamos vivos*.

~

I. Poems of Soledad con Biznagas in Málaga

Biznagas (Malagueñas) is a fresh bouquet of jasmine and a symbol of Málaga.

"Ojalá": *Ojalá* in Spanish means "I hope." According to academics, it derives from the Arabic *wa-sha'allah* or *law sha'allah*. However, most often, people identify ojalá with *Insha'allah*, which means "God willing"—that's how it's reflected in the poem. La Manquita, or "one armed woman," is the name of the Cathedral built between 1528 and 1782. It was, like many churches and cathedrals in Spain, erected on or near a site of a former mosque.

"Walking to the Alcázar": *Alcazaba* in Arabic is *al qasbah*, which means "citadel." *Gibralfaro* or Gebel-faro means "rock of lighthouse"—the first part comes from the Arabic word *yabal*, which means "mountain," and the second part from the Greek word *faruk*, which means "lighthouse." The Alcazaba-Gibralfaro was built in the eleventh century. Airón Well is forty meters deep, carved out of the rock, and is designed in an Arab style. *Chiringuito* is an open-air restaurant.

The Nicaraguan poet Rubén Darío (1867–1916) was the central figure of the literary movement modernismo, which began in Latin America in the late 1800s and spread to Spain, influencing Spanish writers of the first decade of the twentieth century. Modernismo was principally influenced by French symbolism and the Parnassian school of poets, but elements of classical Spanish poetry and the influence of American poets such as Edgar Allen Poe and Walt Whitman could also be found. Darío was an important literary influence on Lorca during his formative years.

"The Wounded Horse and a Tree in an Old Night": When I arrived in Málaga, the city of Pablo Picasso's birth, I wanted to retrace his life. The house where he was born is small and unassuming, and I couldn't feel him anywhere. I could only think of his painting *Guernica*—now at the Museo Nacional Centro de Arte Reina Sofía in Madrid—a response to the bombing in the Basque Country. It is a masterpiece, but it has never been the Picasso painting I have necessarily gone back to over the years. Then it struck me that the horse at the center of the painting was trying to tell me something. I thought of the title of my book of poems, *Love and Strange Horses*, which was just about to come out. But what was the horse trying to say? I didn't figure it out until I was reading the final drafts of the manuscript—that horses to me symbolize an apocalypse, a revelation.

Mudéjar, which comes from the Arabic word *mudajjan* or "domesticated," is the name given to a Moor or Muslim of Al-Andalus who stayed in Christian territory after the Reconquista—when Christian forces drove Muslims from Spain—but who did not convert to Christianity. It also refers to a style of Spanish architecture and décor, particularly of Aragon and Castile, influenced by Islamic traditions between the twelfth and sixteenth centuries.

"Gypsy with a Song": People make literary pilgrimages to Málaga's St. George's Anglican cemetery to visit tombs of well-known authors. At night it is a venue that hosts impromptu jazz sessions. Some lines in the poem are from "Gypsy without a Song" by Duke Ellington. Antigua Casa de Guardia, open since 1840, is a wine bar in Málaga that sells *vino dulce*—such as Pajarete, Moscatel. They have a Mandamientos de Vino listing ten injunctions about wine, the first one being "Amarás el vino sobre todas las cosas" or "love wine above all else." Teatro Cervantes, originally called Teatro de la Libertad, is Málaga's iconic theatre. The Mercado Central de Atarazanas dates back to the fourteenth century, and the rest of it is Neomudéjar—an architectural movement of the nineteenth century inspired by the Mudéjar architecture. It was once a mosque and was named after a gate with an Arab-style arch. The building lacks the original roof that would make it an example of a perfect Arabic bazaar.

"Tomás Heredia, 8": I resided on Tomás Heredia, 8 while living in Málaga. It is in the center of the city. During the day, I often observed the building in front of my window. It was a beautiful edifice, although in disrepair, with molded décor on the façade—like estates by the Mediterranean Sea. A few corners down, a Muslim grocery store owner sold halal meat. And spread throughout the area were cafes thronged with people drinking coffee and eating jamón or boquerones, of course, among many other tapas. And in the blue hours, I saw prostitutes in the far corners—one here, one there—many of them natives of Latin America or Africa. All the contradictions of contemporary Andalucía breathed on those few blocks—the light and dark shades, those enjoying life, those enduring it, those at home, those trying to integrate, those sleeping, those trying to survive. Like in New York City—apart from some extremely wealthy areas—in Málaga there exists a mixture of all kinds of people and lives.

~

Málaga is like the ocean's breath—breezy and delightful. There is something about Málaga that inspires leisure. I was not surprised when people told me that in Andalucía the Malagueños know how to live better than any other people in the region. The city center is not very big; I could walk to most places within fifteen to twenty minutes. I often went to the small but wonderful bookstore Cincoechegaray on calle Echegaray. The people there are among the friendliest I've met, and apart from discussing books and Spanish authors and poets with me, they let me listen to as much old and new flamenco as I wanted and for as long as I wanted. I kept going back to Camarón de la Isla and Joaquín el Canastero. And in the bars, like the famous Bar El Pimpi, amid the clapping glasses and plates, and the noise of people trying to speak to each other, I could still hear the music.

In the cultural district of Málaga, I also discovered an interesting bookstore, Librería Proteo. During Muslim Spain, the city had different doors or gates, and a piece of the wall of the Buenaventura door or Bab al-Jawja is now part of the store. Visiting there is like entering a museum of time: a wall from Islamic Spain, books with old and new covers, a bookseller with tattoos all over his arm.

Not far is the amazing Centro Cultural Generación del 27, where I spent a lot of time reading, drinking coffee, and speaking to poets and literary people. The poet Aurora Luque is the director of the center. I met her along with Julio Neira, director of the Centro Andaluz de las Letras (and most recently, director general del Libro, Archivos y Bibliotecas, Consejería de Cultura, Junta de Andalucía), and Rafael Ballesteros at Dickinson College in 2008 during the international festival Semana Poética. I was introduced to the novelist Antonio Soler by Grace Jarvis, who directed the Dickinson College-Málaga program. Antonio and I discussed the controversy in Spain concerning the Law of Historical Memory—those who want to revisit the crimes committed during the Franco era and get compensation for their suffering, and those who are against revisiting it. While I was there different locations were being dug up for the remains of those assassinated, including those of Lorca. Being passionate about photography and *what remains*, I took pictures of many of the assassination sites.

I found numerous images worth capturing in this city. One such image arose while I was sitting in a restaurant facing a window with the Christmas lights hanging in front of the glass like small fires, overlooking Plaza de la Merced. The gray skies reflecting on the square, the buildings painted in yellow, the rain just ending. Click. Within minutes, another click, another image, a light blue sky with a few clouds, buildings that seemed to be yellow are actually white, with only the contours of the windows painted yellow. And the small fires were now reflecting on the cobblestones.

Throughout Spain there are paradores—luxurious state-owned hotels, many of which are historic buildings (medieval castles, former palaces, convents, monasteries, or fortresses). From the Parador de Málaga Gibralfaro I could see the entire city. The seaport and the misty pink skies reminded me of Cádiz, of being somewhere in Beirut or Jaffa. I thought of all those who arrived and then left here, making me wonder if I too was just passing by.

One day as I was walking among Málaga's dark, musky, and narrow alleys, with clothes hanging from balconies that created an opening to a vast blue, my eyes fell on a quote by Luis de Góngora y Argote written on one of the walls: "Los ojos con mucha noche" (The eyes full of night). And then a little further down, under a window a quote from José Moreno Villa: "Ni al cielo ni al mar llegan las coplas de los hombres" (Neither from the sky nor from the sea come the verses of men). And finally at the curve, on a faded yellow wall one line from Konstantinos Kavafis: "No hallarás otra tierra ni otro mar. La ciudad irá en ti siempre." (You won't find a new country, won't find another shore. This city will always pursue you). This made me think of Ibn Zamrak, el Poeta de la Alhambra, whose poems are on the walls and around the edges of the fountains of the Alhambra.

Málaga province is formed of one hundred towns. The translator Alberto López, who became a close friend and the best guide I could ask for, took me to as many towns as possible, among them Fuengirola, Torrox, Mijas, Marbella, Nerja, Ronda, Torremolinos, and Frigiliana. We saw the Guadalhorce River and La Peña de los Enamorados (the Lovers' Leap), Carratraca, El Chorro (the lake district), El Camino del Rey, the Pink Lagoon. On the way, we stopped at an abandoned *cortijo*, and the soil around the farmhouse was orange brown. In Antequera, the sunset was mesmerizing as the light sat on the mountaintop before it departed, something I often observed in the small Andalusian towns. And when the sun was gone but it wasn't dark yet, with the sky bluer than I can describe and the lights turned on in houses, I found a certain magic. But of all these places, one in particular stays with me—Comares. As we drove up the hill higher and higher, passing olives and lemon trees, pines and eucalyptus, I left pieces of myself in the landscape. There, time was redefining itself or Comares was redefining time. There, mountains gather spirits. It is where trees show their souls to those who want to see.

II. *Maktoub*, the Moor Said

"*Maktoub*, the Moor Said": The section title comes from a book by the explorer, Edward Rae (1847–1923), *The Country of the Moors: A Journey from*

Tripoli in Barbary to the City of Kairwân (London: John Murray, Albemarle Street, 1877), which speaks of his travels from Tripoli, in present-day Libya, to the holy city of Kairouan (Kairwan) in modern Tunisia. Rae was one of the earliest non-Muslims to write about these cities, including their Jewish quarters. As I was reading, I found this quote, which reflects what the Moors as well as new immigrants from North Africa, Latin America, and elsewhere coming to Spain generally feel today: "We asked some of the Moors what they would do if the steamer sailed for Tunis without landing them. *Maktoub*, they said, good naturedly. It is written" (162).

"El País": In Spanish, *fulano* means "what's-his-name" or "someone without a name"—whoever. It derives from the Arabic *fulan*.

"Tree of Red Leaves, Jaén 2009": The general and dictator Francisco Franco was head of Spain from 1939 until 1975.

"Paraguas Perdido": Ecuadorians are the largest group of Latin Americans in Spain. *Vega* in Spanish means a "plain" or "valley"—the Spanish meaning of vega applies throughout this book.

"The Courtyard of Colegiata del Salvador": In Granada, Albayzín is the old Moorish quarter of the city, facing the Alhambra. Today's Albayzín used to be the Alcazaba, the Moorish citadel, and the oldest part of the Alhambra. The courtyard of what was once the Albayzín's great mosque is now attached to the church of the Colegiata del Salvador. The *adhan* is the Muslim call to prayer. Moroccans form one of the largest groups of immigrants in Spain.

"Sacromonte": Sacromonte is a neighborhood of Granada and is the Gitano quarter of the city. Gitanos are the Romani people in Spain, who migrated out of the Indian subcontinent west into Europe around the eleventh century. I went to Sacromonte by foot, and when I arrived, the view from the hill was in communion with the music of the place.

III. Alleys and Reveries

"Only one voice, in the distance, / always heard in the distance, / accompanies it and makes it move / the way the neck moves with the shoulders" wrote Miguel Hernández, from *Recent Poetry of Spain*, translated and edited by Louis Hammer and Sara Schyfter (Old Chatham, New York: Sachem Press, 1983), 20–21.

"Christmas in Benalmádena": Turrón is nougat, a confection made of fruits and nuts in a sugar paste. I went to my friend Alberto López's house on Christmas Eve; his family treated me as family, and of course, we had more dinner courses than I can remember. Later on, I went to a small bar off of Calle Larios for drinks and to listen to flamenco. The next day I celebrated Christmas in the quaint café Puerta Oscura, open since 1991.

"Now That": The cover of the December 2009 magazine *Zoom Málaga* featured the legendary singer and poet Joaquín Sabina. After a silence of four years, he had just released a new album, *Vinagre y rosas*. Sabina has always taken me places to dream, along with Léo Ferré, Charles Aznavour, Georges Moustaki, Georges Brassens, and Leonard Cohen. The well-known Spanish poet Luis García Montero, who is one of Sabina's good friends, wrote the introduction to his CD. This poem was inspired by the song, "Ahora que."

Lorca came to poetry through music. Two important poets in his life, Machado and Unamuno, were singers of the Castilian countryside. (I myself have often collaborated with musicians.) Although Lorca did not study music, he never stopped playing the piano or singing. In various parts of the book, I explore the poem as song or as a form melodic enough that it could be sung. Music is a personage or the humming shadow in the book.

~

I can't get enough of the *teterías* or "tea houses," los baños árabes or "Arab baths" throughout Andalucía as well as the white villages and caballo andaluz.

IV. Constelación en el Ateneo de Sevilla

"Seven Stars in Sevilla": In December 1927, a tribute was held in the Ateneo de Sevilla to mark the three-hundredth anniversary of the death of the Baroque poet Luis de Góngora y Argote. Rafael Alberti, Gerardo Diego, Juan Chabas, Dámaso Alonso, Jorge Guillén, Jóse Bergamín, and Federico García Lorca traveled together by train to Sevilla. They became known as "el siete de la fama," also known as the generation of '27. There were two poets missing on the trip: Pedro Salinas and Vicente Aleixandre. The other poets who joined the seven poets in the Ateneo and also considered part of the generation of '27 were Luis Cernuda, Fernando Villalón, Rafael Laffón, Adriano del Valle, and Joaquín Romero Murube. The patron of the trip and of this celebration of Góngora was the famous bullfighter Ignacio Sánchez Mejías (elegized by Lorca in "Llanto por la muerte de Ignacio Sánchez Mejías," "Lament for the Death of Ignacio Sánchez Mejías"). These poets were not the only ones considered as the generation of '27; among many others were Manuel Altolaguirre and Emilio Prados.

After the reading in the Ateneo de Sevilla, the poets went to the outskirts of Sevilla where Ignacio Sánchez Mejías threw a party in his estate, La Finca de Pino Montano. The guests wore *djellabas* or traditional long, loose-fitting Arab robes. Manuel Torre, the great Gypsy *cantaor*, who Lorca met in 1922 at the Festival de Cante Jondo in Granada that was lead by maestro Manuel de Falla, captivated the guests as he sang with great *duende*.

In 1936, Unamuno was placed in house arrest and died a few months later. In 1939, Machado died in exile, in the French bordertown of Collioure. Miguel Hernández was imprisoned and sentenced to death. He died in prison in 1942. Vicente Aleixandre had a kidney operation in 1936 that left him bedridden and incapable of leaving Madrid during the conflict (he won the Nobel Prize in Literature in 1977 and died in 1984). Rafael Alberti was exiled to Argentina, Luis Cernuda to Mexico, Juan Ramón Jiménez to Puerto Rico, and Pedro Salinas and Jorge Guillén to the United States.

~

Translation of quotes from "Seven Stars in Sevilla":

Where is paradise, my shadows, you that were there? A silent question? Rafael Alberti, from "Paraíso Perdido," *Sobre los ángeles.*

There will be a green silence, all made of unstrung guitars. The guitar is well filled with wind instead of water. Gerardo Diego, from "Guitarra."

No, love, nobody knows; nobody, not even you, my love, know I'm waiting with you. . . . Juan Chabás, from "Esta noche es tan honda y es tan larga."

When I killed you, you were looking outside at my garden. This clear December presses on me its colors and light. Dámaso Alonso, from "Elegía a un Moscardón Azul."

The world fits into our forgetting. Jorge Guillén, from *Horses in the Air and Other Poems,* translated by Cola Franzen.

The only reality I have is the unreality of time. José Bergamín, from "Tres Sonetos a Cristo Crucificado Ante El Mar (# 21)," *Antología Poética.*

Soledad Montoya, let peace into your heart. Federico García Lorca, from "Romance de la pena negra" ("Ballad of Black Pain"). Lorca read "A Ballad of Dark Sorrow" and other poems from *Gypsy Ballads* in the Ateneo de Sevilla.

~

The view from the Guadalquivir and the Puente de Isabel II alone makes visiting Sevilla worth it as well as the creations of the tremendous architect Anibal González Álvarez-Ossorio (1876–1929). Some of his masterpieces include the one in Plaza de España, made of face brick (ladrillo visto) with applications of polychrome ceramic, and the Palacio de Arte Antiguo, el Pabellón Real, and el Palacio de Bellas Artes.

Sevilla took me back to my ancestral hometown, and Lorca's poem "Joke about Don Pedro on Horseback," where Sevilla is mingled with Bethlehem: "A city of gold in a forest of cedar. / Is it Bethlehem?" It was also in Sevilla that I began to comprehend what had happened in Haiti—where I lived for numerous years—in the January 12 earthquake. For two days after the disaster, I had no information. I called everyone I knew: my sister and cousins in London, my other cousin in Paris, my parents in the Dominican Republic, my friend Edwidge Dandicat in Miami, and Haitians I knew in New York. They provided me with no information or contradictory news. Those two days were excruciating. It had been over twenty years since I had been in Haiti for any length of time, with only a few very short visits during those two decades. But I still knew many people there. Suddenly, childhood memories came flooding back of people and places I hadn't seen but would hear news about over the years; Rosanna and Anita who helped my grandmother in her pastry shop; Gregory, the Haitian boy my grandmother helped raise. And I thought about Port-au-Prince—the city as I knew it, was gone. While I was in Sevilla news was starting to come in. The name of the dead piling up in my heart, and I did not know what to do with my grief. Lorca's line "a las cinco de la tarde" or "at five in the afternoon," kept coming to mind. And I wrote and wrote—poems I have not yet published.

Later I thought about this circle of my life. I had left Haiti soon after Duvalier was ousted in 1986 and discovered Lorca not long afterward. And now here I was in Lorca's homeland, rediscovering my memories of Haiti and knowing that my next journey had to be a long overdue visit to the island. But the same question keeps persisting, whether I am thinking of the Middle East, Haiti, or Africa: how do I reconcile myself with the shadows that death leaves behind?

V. In Córdoba

"Alhandal y las Murallas de Córdoba": Córdoba has always had a vivid place in my imagination. It reminds me of the old city of Jerusalem. It was once known for its thriving and multicultural community consisting of Muslim, Jewish, and Christian artists, writers, scholars and philosophers. The area around the Mezquita, which means "mosque" in Spanish, now called the Mezquita-catedral, is today one of the most impressive examples of Spain's Moorish heritage. Nothing adequately describes the mosque-cathedral. The red and white columns are one of the most beautiful creations I've ever seen. It is mystifying.

While I was there, I saw an announcement for a Spanish rock group, Alhándal. The spelling of the name, which I had seen previously only in Bethlehem, intrigued me. I decided to find out where these Spanish boys found this name and if my name meant the same thing in Spanish as in Arabic—bitter medicinal plant. Indeed, alhandal derives from the Arabic and is a name for colocynth. Alhandal was sold in Arab pharmacies in Islamic Spain. The colocynth is also known as bitter apple, bitter cucumber, or vine of Sodom. The plant is native to the Mediterranean basin and Asia.

Ibn Zaydun (1003–1070, Córdoba), Ibn Hazm (994–1063, Córdoba), Ibn Faraj (tenth century Jaén), Ibn Iyad (1083–1149, Central Andalucía), and Ibn Sharaf (d. 1068, Qayrawan), were Arab Andalusian poets; Francisco Gómez de Quevedo (1580–1645, Madrid), Luis de Góngora y Argote (1561–1627, Córdoba), Garcilaso de la Vega (c. 1501–1536), Lope de Vega (1562–1635) were writers of the Spanish Golden Age.

Zahara de la Sierra is a small town in the province of Cádiz in the hills of Andalucía; Bab al-Yawz, now Almodóvar Gate, leads to the Judería. Maimónides (1134–1204) is one of Judaism's greatest thinkers. The Sinagoga or synagogue was built in 5075 in the Jewish calendar, which is 1314–1315 in Christian era.

In the Plaza del Potro is Posada del Potro, the inn cited by Cervantes in *Don Quijote*. During the Middle Ages and Renaissance the squares were where public executions took place.

Mesbahas are prayer beads. Oviedo is the capital city of the Principality of Asturias in northern Spain.

Andalucía is home to a variety of wildflowers, including sea lavenders, crown daisies, wild gladiolus, grey leaved cistuses, and bishop's weed.

Miguel de Unamuno (1864–1936) was an essayist, novelist, poet, playwright, and philosopher from Bilbao, Biscay, Basque Country.

Zajal is a genre of vernacular strophic poetry that established itself as a literary form around 1100 in al-Andalus and is still popular in various parts of the Arab world. Zajal is the vernacular form of the *muwashshah*, an Andalusian Arabic strophic form that seemed to have developed from

Romance folk poetry and was adopted in the eleventh century by the Hebrew poets. *Kharja* means "closure" or "ending" in Arabic and is the final couplet of the secular muwashshah. The muwashshah was sung.

"10 Qit'as": *Qit'a* means "fragment." It is a short poem in the Arabic tradition, up to ten or twenty lines in English, which tends to concentrate on a single subject or theme. It is thought to have "broken off" from a longer poetic form, the *qasida*.

Statistics vary concerning the percentage of Spanish words that derive from the Arabic—anywhere between 5 to 20 percent.

"Patios": Patios are popular in Córdoba. In the springtime there is a patio contest.

~

To commemorate the seventieth anniversary of the beginning of the exile of Spanish artists as a result of the aftermath of the Spanish Civil War and later World War II, an exhibition entitled *Después de la Alambrada: 1939–1960* was being presented in the Sala Museística Cajasur and Palacio de la Merced. I discovered Spanish visual artists in exile in the Americas and Europe. Some of the artists who immigrated to Mexico I knew already, such as Remedios Varo and Miguel Prieto. But so many others were unknown to me such as Elvira Gascón, the only woman in the many well-known artists who went to Mexico. I was also unaware of those artists who lived at some point in exile in Santo Domingo, where my brother has resided for close to two decades, like Eugenio Granell, Vela Zanetti, and Joan Junyer. Many went to France, namely Manuel Viola, Baltasar Lobo, Óscar Domínguez (whose work *Fuego de estrellas*, or *Fire of Stars*, was being exhibited in Picasso's house), and Leandre Cristfol, who had also lived in Morocco.

Also, the grand beauty of Madinat al-Zahra, a Muslim medieval town about five kilometers from Córdoba took me by surprise.

When I arrived in Córdoba I was elated. This city brought back memories of family and of the Middle East—the orange trees in the courtyard reminded me of having afternoon coffee in the American Colony Hotel in Jerusalem; going to the Salón de Té on Buen Pastor, 13, and seeing Café Maatouk reminded me of Lebanon and of my grandmother. Amid all these vivid Córdoban places are also contradictions: an ice cream sign beside an Islamic door, a church where a mosque once stood not far from an iron gate advertising Brugal, el Ron de los Dominicanos, and on the front cover of *El País* the headline "ETA intentó derribar tres veces el avión de Aznar con un misil" followed by a photo of the president and his wife in 3-D glasses watching *Avatar* with a note, "El president Montilla echa un pulso al cine de Hollywood."

VI. By the Door, or Is It Death

"Dado": In Spanish, *dado* is the singular of dice. It stems from the classical Arabic *a'dad*, which means "numbers."

"La Guerra": Radiocadena Española (RCE) consisted of stations formerly owned by Franco groups.

VII. Granada

"Sheets of Dry Winds": *Chopos* are poplars.

~

Lorca was born in Fuente Vaqueros on June 5, 1898, and was killed in 1936. I am not sure what I expected when I arrived on the street—now called Manuel de Falla—where the poet was born. It was mostly poor and inhabited by Gypsies. I suppose that might be appropriate in a way. Alberto and I had coffee at the café-bar El Reloj, and then headed to Valderrubio where Lorca's father had a farmhouse and where Lorca lived before his family moved to Granada. I discovered that Valderrubio was once named Qariat al Sakruya (tenth and eleventh century), then Wadi Askuruya, then Axxacucha or Axcorocha (fourteenth century), Escuraja (1431), Ascorosa (1501), Asquerosa (1592), Acuerosa (1887), Asquerosa again (1897), Maria Cristina (1931), and finally Valderrubio (1943).

Then we went to Alfacar and Víznar where Lorca was killed and where the earth was still open from the search for Lorca's bones as well as the remains of others killed with him. Nothing was found. For some reason all I could think about was Rafael Alberti's painting *Estampa del sur* (1924) in Lorca's Huerta de San Vicente in Granada. This image of the south, which Alberti dedicated to the beginning of their friendship, depicts a man in a red cap looking up at a gray fortress. Above the fortress, small colorful flags form a triangle with a faceless Madonna wearing yellow and holding a child in red. My eyes kept going back to that suspended triangle. I didn't understand Alberti's message to Lorca but the image was so alive in contrast to the open mounds of earth I had just seen in Alfacar and Víznar.

Walking on the hills of this glorious place, I found it difficult to believe so many bodies are buried underneath. It's quiet and uneasy. The landscape speaks to me but death only pretends to have a language. And so do the small streams that thread through the terrain.

The vistas on the way to Granada always have an indescribable effect on me. The endless olive trees, the dramatic skies. Here are the Sierra Nevada's two highest peaks the Veleta (3,395 meters) and the Mulhacén (3,479 meters)—named after Abu Hasan Ali or Muley Hacén as he is known in Spanish, a fifteenth century Muslim King of Granada. There is a myth that he was buried on the summit of the mountain. Below, the elegant beauty of the Alpujarra valleys. And then of course, the Alhambra at the heart of Granada. The morning mist circling the palace fills the soul, tells us the secret of magic. But it asks us to explain and we can't, all we can do is be with it.

There is so much here: the view of the snow-covered mountains, the Darro valley, the pines, the white houses and their tile rooftops like small hats, and the music of the water flowing through the city, mostly there is a song and everyone of us has to find it our own way.

Did Washington Irving find his? He left us with his book *The Alhambra* (1832), which chronicles his sojourn in Spain, but what else did he find while living in the Alhambra (which seems like a surreal experience today especially if you are standing in his room) that he kept to himself? I went to see the exhibition entitled *Washington Irving y la Alhambra, 150 Aniversario (1858–2009)*, and I felt, more than ever, how captivated Irving was with the magnificence of this place. Why couldn't such splendor unite our silences?

VIII. Convivencia

"Awon / Sin": *Awon* is Aramaic and appears frequently throughout the Old Testament and in parallel with other words related to sin, such as *chatta'th* and *pesha'*. In Hebrew it is spelled Avon.

"Convivencia / Two Ghazals Two Tzvis": *Convivencia* in Spanish means "coexistence." The Spanish convivencia describes the time when Christians, Jews, and Muslims lived in relative harmony in Islamic Spain. There are numerous debates surrounding notions of tolerance in al-Andalus during the Middle Ages. However, one cannot deny the rich and prosperous cultural and artistic life that existed during that period—a life that these communities created together. As I was writing this section, Mahmoud Darwish's words kept echoing: "Andalus . . . might be here or there, or anywhere . . .

a meeting place of strangers in the project of building human culture. . . . It is not only that there was a Jewish-Muslim coexistence, but that the fates of the two people were similar. . . . Al-Andalus for me is the realization of the dream of the poem."

In Arabic, *ghazal* refers to a poem dealing with the theme of love, whether long, medium, short, verse, prose, and so on. The Hebrew equivalent of the *ghazal* is the *tzvi* or *tzviyah, ya'ala* or *ofer*, which also means a "roe" or "gazelle" (Song of Songs 4:5, "Thy two breasts [are] like two young roes that are twins, which feed among the lilies"). The proper Hebrew term would be *shirei heshek* (which literally means "poems of desire").

"Ghazal / 2": This ghazal is inspired by Lorca's "Ghazal VII—Ghazal of the Memory of Love," where all lines end with o. Additionally, I wanted to alternate between a Spanish and an English word that ends with o.

Albérchigo means a "clingstone apricot" or "peach," from the Andalusi Arabic *albershiq; cero* or *zero*, from *sifr* of the same meaning. *Algarazo* means a "short rainstorm," possibly from the Arabic *algazeer*, which means "heavy rain." *Diwan* is a collection of poetry (Arabic, Persian, or Urdu). *Azulejo* means "bluish," from the Arabic word *zullayj*, and it is a form of Portuguese or Spanish painted, glazed tilework. *Zoco* or *azogue* means "market," from the Arabic *souk* with the same meaning.

"Abásho": *Abásho* means "what's below" or "the departed" in Ladino. Ladino, also called Judeo-Spanish, is a Romance language derived from late medieval Spanish with elements of Hebrew, Turkish, Arabic, Aramaic, French, Italian, and Greek (written using the Hebrew alphabet). It was spoken by Sephardic Jews in the former Ottoman Empire. Today, Ladino is nearly extinct. Only one high school in Jerusalem has a Ladino language program, and there is little new literature being produced in the language. It is similar to modern Spanish in the same way that Yiddish is similar to modern German.

"The Book of Toledo": Saffron, one of the most sensuous of spices is grown in this region. Its intense golden yellow-red color and flavor are seductive. Without it, two of my favorite dishes wouldn't exist: paella and bouillabaisse. Some of my best memories of Spain come from my time in Toledo, which I visited while at university and often afterward. One incident in particular stays with me. It occurred while I was visiting my sister Alexandra, who was living there in the mid-1990s. We were walking the twisted streets, stopped to watch some men play briscas (a popular Spanish card game), and were discussing the mesmerizing plains of La Mancha when an old lady gave us a postcard featuring a black-and-white photo of what seemed a field or a plain. When we looked closer we could see an image of a small book on the grass. The old lady left and we continued walking, not thinking much of the encounter. Years later, during one of my many moves, I found a photo of my sister and me sitting on the steps of a tiny store, laughing; stuck to it was the postcard. I thought of how free we felt that day and how lucky I was to have had that feeling even for a moment. After all, Toledo represented to some extent coexistence between Jews and Muslims. Yet at the time I found the postcard, the Palestinian-Israeli conflict was getting worse (with the start of the second Intifada). And because I don't think anything is a coincidence, I wondered what the encounter with the old lady meant. When I was in Toledo recently, the photo and postcard came to mind, and I felt an urgent need to see them. Returning to New York, I looked for them in my trunk of images. Days later, I found the photo but never found the postcard. This poem was inspired by what I might have read in that book (and written after a chain of proverbs and stone carvings from *Butterfly Valley* by Sherko Bekas, translated by Choman Hardi).

IX. Flight to Catalunya and Afternoons in Galicia

"Wandering, fugitive, mysterious, / the clouds take their swift flight," from "To My Mother (1863)" by Rosalía de Castro, translated by Michael Smith.

Rosalía de Castro (1837–1885) was a revolutionary Galician poet and writer. Lorca and Cernuda, among many others, praised her work in the twentieth century. Today, she is recognized as one of the most important writers in Galician and Spanish. Her work along with the work of few other poets is considered the beginning of modern Galician poetry. After her death, her eldest daughter destroyed her unpublished manuscripts, at the poet's request.

"Quartet in Catalunya": *Ara* means "now" in Catalan. When you are reading the poem, start with *now* before every stanza. La Rambla is a famous street in Barcelona. Its name derives from the Arabic *raml* and is a seasonal stream that once ran outside the city walls until the fourteenth century. La Sagrada Familia is a church built by the legendary architect Antoni Gaudí. It is one of the most awe-striking monuments I've ever seen. Tibidabo is the highest hill forming the backdrop in Barcelona. It gets its name from the passage in the Latin Vulgate Bible in which the devil, trying to tempt Christ, takes him to a high place and says, "I will give you all of this, if you fall down and worship me."

∼

I flew from Málaga to Barcelona and met the British-Sudanese novelist Jamal Mahjoub, the writer and *Guernica Magazine* editor Michael Archer, and graphic designers Rosa Mercader and Tere Guix. Barcelona is one of my favorite cities. I fell in love with it the first time I visited back in the early nineties. The city is vibrant, and Gaudí's buildings are its centerpieces. We eventually drove from Barcelona to L'Armentera.

In the days that followed, I explored more than a dozen villages and towns in the area—such as Ventalló, Montiró, L'Escala, and Empúries, where the Greek ruins are. I took photographs every day. During one of the sunsets, I took images of a blue sky with pink clouds, and within minutes the clouds turned deep gray above a huge flame. Finally, I headed to Figueres where I went to see the Teatre-Museu Dalí before heading back to Málaga.

~

"Waltz of a Dream": Written like a song. It was inspired by Leonard Cohen's "Take this Waltz," which was inspired by Lorca's "Little Viennese Waltz."

"Santiago": The grave of Santiago Apóstel (St. James the Apostle) was *rediscovered* in 813 at what became Santiago de Compostela. Thousands of pilgrims come to Santiago de Compostela to walk the Camino de Santiago. The faithful believe that Santiago Apóstel preached in Galicia and was buried there. They think that after his death in Palestine he was brought back by stone boat. The Catedral de Santiago de Compostela is the spiritual pulse of the city. In the portico's central archway is a figure of Christ enthroned as described in the Book of Revelation. Surrounding him are the four evangelists, angels, and symbols of Jesus' passion, and in the arc above are the twenty-four musicians who are said to surround the throne. Below Christ's feet is Santiago and below him Hercules, who is holding open the mouths of two lions. The cathedral's Holy Door, or Puerta Santa, opens up to the Praza da Quintana. The line "too much of the wrong heart on the wrong road" was inspired by lines in Lorca's poem, "Little Infinite Poem," dedicated to Luis Cardoza y Aragón.

~

I met the Galician poet Yolanda Castaño in Caracas, Venezuela, a few years before I started writing this book. She inspired me to explore Galicia but every time I was to go, something forestalled my trip. It was meant to unfold this way because years later I finished *Poet in Andalucía* in Santiago de Compostela. It was also in Galicia that I started preparing the second part of my journey, my trip to Buenos Aires and the many other places Lorca went to after New York. It was in Buenos Aires that Lorca grew increasingly interested in Galicia, after having met many Galician exiles and immigrants there. Coincidentally and amusingly, the Fundación Araguaney—named after the national tree of Venezuela and founded by the Galician-Arab Ghaleb Jaber—made my journey to Galicia possible with its generous support.

Ghaleb Jaber Martínez (son of Ghaleb Jaber) is one of the main forces behind the foundation, which is an impressive creative space for Spanish, Galician, Latin American, and Arab literature, film, music, and visual art. Its presence is important, and it continues to expose me to a vast array of creative minds.

Arriving in Santiago de Compostela—a World Heritage Site and one of the three capitals of Christianity along with Jerusalem and Rome—was like entering a dream city where fantasy and reality merge and submerge. The city has secrets and makes sure we know it. It has mysterious beats and enjoys watching us try to discover them. It looks like nowhere else in Spain I visited. It's green, so green it at once blinds and bestows vision. The old town is small but grand. In the outskirts, at the top of Mount Gaiás, is the City of Culture of Galicia designed by the American architect Peter Eisenman. Built to host arts and cultural activities and to preserve the heritage of the region, it is a modern stone and glass building, indeed like a "city" mirroring the historical quarter of Compostela. And finally, the small deities of Santiago are the chimneys. They are iconic elements of the cityscape.

The Roman past of this area is evident in its name, Galicia, which derives from Gallaecia, the province established by Rome in the northwestern part of the peninsula. The Celtic feel floats in the air. The beaches, forests, coves, and forts mesmerize. Galicians are passionate about the Atlantic and its coast. Other unforgettable places I visited in the region: Lugo Wall (in Lugo)—the only Roman wall that is completely preserved—the Rías Bajas (Low Estuaries), Finisterre, and, of course, the Camino de Santiago or the Way of St. James, which attracts pilgrims worldwide. I couldn't resist going to the magnificently melancholic city of Oporto in Portugal, which is only a few hours away from Galicia.

While in Galicia, a disconcerting incident occurred. The Códice Calixtino—the twelfth-century illustrated manuscript described as the first travel guidebook of Europe—vanished from the Cathedral of Santiago de Compostela. How could such a theft occur? The historical and illuminated codex was a collection of texts, including sermons, a guide to the pilgrimage routes to Santiago, and told the story of how St. James the Apostle's body got to northwestern Spain. After this regretful occurrence, I could almost inhale *la morriña* in the air —a term used by Galicians, and known to be present in Castro's work, to signify nostalgia, especially for the land. The Portuguese say *saudade*. Galicia and Northern Portugal share this common melancholic spirit.

Galicia seduced me into creating dream cities in the arc of my spirit. The last line in *Poet in New York* is, "I'm going to Santiago." Although, Lorca was going to a different Santiago (his was Cuba), we both found a certain *ending* in Santiago.

X. The Poet Arrives in Tangier and Afterward

I took the fast boat from Tarifa to Tangier. As much as I love the sea, I don't enjoy being on boats. In about two hours, I arrived. Tangier floats through you. The city escapes you as if it wants you to pursue it. I called Sean, and he could only meet me in the evening. But he suggested I come to the Cinémathèque de Tanger on Place du 9 Avril 1947 (Cinéma Rif, Grand Socco, 90000 Tanger), a restored art house that he bought and runs.

I made my way to the cinémathèque, and what an unbelievable restoration. I could feel the vibrant energy of young people as they wrote on their computers and socialized over tea. Then I went around the corner to Darna, Rue Jules Cot, Place du 9 Avril, to eat. It is a women's center with a wonderful courtyard that serves lunch (mostly couscous). What makes this place special is that its profits help women and children. There is also a store that sells artwork made by women. In the afternoon, I walked the alleys and intersections and passed the arches through the medina. This place has aged and is ageless. The antennas and faded colors of houses— pink, yellow, blue, stand out.

In the evening, I meet Sean. We passed some cafés where only men are allowed and where they drink lots of coffee and very sweet mint tea. We then headed for a drink at Number One, an absolutely wonderful bar-restaurant that feels like the 1960s. Kareem, the owner, greeted us and we spoke to him for a while.

A few hours later, I left Sean, and I went to the El Minzah Hotel, 85, Rue de La Liberté, Tangier. I passed the old courtyard to get to Caid's Piano Bar. A few foreigners linger at the bar, with a man on the piano. I picked up a catalog of the hotel featuring Rock Hudson, Rita Hayworth, and Aristotle Onassis.

That evening, as I looked at the turquoise walls of my room at the Dar Nour guesthouse in the Kasbah, I thought of the great traveler Ibn Battuta

(1304–1368), who was born in Tangier, and wondered what he thought about in the late hours of the nights while he was journeying.

Before leaving the room in the morning, I went to the balcony and stood there for a while. One of Paul Bowles's lines kept coming back to me: "Security is a false god: begin making sacrifices to it and you are lost" (from "Notes Mailed at Nagercoil").

And as I was about to leave, my eyes fell on a quote by Marcel Proust: "Le seul véritable voyage, le seul bain de Jouvence, ce ne serait pas d'aller vers de nouveaux paysages, mais d'avoir d'autres yeux, de voir l'univers avec les yeux d'un autre, de cent autres, de voir les cent univers que chacun d'eux voit, que chacun d'eux est."

~

"Tanger Bleu": *Bakhshish* in Arabic means "gratuity"; *medina* means "city"; *djellaba* is a hooded and sleeved overgarment; *kif* is the frequently used name for hashish in Morocco; *Allah Akhbar* means "Allah is great"; *bled* in North Africa colloquially refers to "countryside" or "hometown"; *qsbah* is a large reed transverse flute with a low register found in the extreme east of Morocco and the western part of the Algerian Sahara—decades ago it was the favorite instrument of the camel drivers.

Café Central in the Petit Socco is one of the places Tennessee Williams, William S. Burroughs, Allen Ginsberg, and others from the Beat generation hung out.

Mohamed Choukri (1935–2003) is a North African author from Tangier, most known for his autobiography *Al-khoubz Al-Hafi* (*For Bread Alone*), translated into English by Paul Bowles. He met Paul Bowles, Jean Genet, and Tennessee Williams in Tangier in the 1960s.

"La Movida": La Movida Madrileña, or La Movida, was headed by Enrique Tierno Galván, a former university professor who was an opposition figure under Franco and affectionately known in Spain as "the old teacher." After the death of Franco in 1975, nothing was taboo for the Madrileños. Galván became the mayor of Madrid in 1979 and was the most popular leader the city has known. La Movida was an artistic and sociocultural movement. Many Spanish figures in the arts rose from La Movida, such as the film director Pedro Almodóvar.

While in Madrid I also visited the Residencia de Estudiantes, which Lorca attended along with his close friends Luis Buñuel and Salvador Dalí, among others. Other important literary figures from an earlier generation who attended and who were significant in Lorca's life include Juan Ramón Jiménez and Miguel de Unamuno.

"On My Way to Tamarit": Tamarit means "rich in dates" in Arabic. It was also the name of the *huerta* or "small farm" that belonged to the father of one of Lorca's favorite cousins. *No puedo verte* in Spanish and *la astati'u an araka* in Arabic mean, "I can't see you."

What I could see was the majesty around me. What I did see was all that coexists. Maybe that's "what we speak of when we speak alone" (García Valdés)—what we are capable of.

~

Lorca wrote, "We Latins want sharp profiles and visible mystery. Form and sensuality." That was one of the things he wanted to accomplish when he wrote *Poet in New York*. And that's what I hope to have delivered in *Poet in Andalucía*. I still keep before me a black-and-white photo of Lorca in a white *djellaba* with a white turban, sitting, and looking straight at whoever decides to look back at him. Lorca said, "Lo que más me importa, es vivir." On this journey, I discovered peace is there if we want to find it, because as was true for Lorca, what people want most is to live.

Acknowledgments

SINCERE THANKS TO the editors and staff of the following publications in which the following poems previously appeared, sometimes in earlier versions:

Guardian ("Awon / Sin"); *Northwest Review* ("The Wounded Horse, and a Tree in an Old Night," and "The Book of Toledo"); *Connotation Press: An Online Artifact* ("Walking to the Alcázar" and "Paraguas Perdido"); *Molossus: World Poetry Portfolio* 21 ("Tomás Heredia, 8," "On the Way to Jerez de la Frontera," "Sheets of Dry Wind," and "Patios"); *Rattapallax Magazine* 19 (Fall 2011) ("10 Qit'as," "Convivencia / Two Ghazals Two Tzvis," excerpt from "Seven Stars in Sevilla," and "Abásho"); Rattapallax Films ("While Waiting for Death," excerpts from "Alhandal y las Murallas de Córdoba" and "Seven Stars in Sevilla"); Women's eNews ("The Thing about Feathers"); *Tongue: A Journal of Writing & Art* ("El Pais," "Dado," and "Ojalá"); *World Literature Today* ("Tree of Red Leaves," "La Guerra," "The Courtyard of Colegiata del Salvador," and "Prophet in Andalucia"); *Thrush Poetry Journal* ("The Moor," "Santiago," "La Movida," and "Waltz of a Dream"); *Black Renaissance Noire* ("Tanger Bleu," "Gypsy with a Song," "On My Way to Tamarit," "Christmas in Benalmádena," and "Testament in Barcelona.")

This book of poetry started with the incredible support of Dickinson College where I was writer-in-residence both in Pennsylvania and Málaga, Spain, in 2009 and 2010.

Deepest thanks to my sponsors: Centro Cultural Generación del 27 and Aurora Luque; Centro Andaluz de las Letras and the Junta de Andalucía, Julio Neira in particular; Fundación Araguaney in Galicia, especially Ghaleb Jaber, who has been incredibly generous.

I am intensely grateful to all those who supported this book and my vision: Dean Neil B. Weissman, Grace L. Jarvis, Ed Webb, Marcelo J. Borges, Bryan Bartosik-Vélez, Brian Brubaker, and Glen Paterson of Dickinson College; Hilary Henglert, Mohsen Emadi, Christopher Merrill, Willis Barnstone, Josip Novakovich, Afaa Weaver, Fred D'Aguiar, David Unger,

Peter Cole, Lorraine Adams, Yolanda Castaño, Veronika Handal, Rana Kazkaz, Najwan Darwish, Tina Chang, Beverly Archer, and Robert Bernard. A very special *gracias* to Ram Devineni, Claudia Gasparini, Abed Ismael, Beverly Rego, Jorge Sagastume, and Marie-Claude Peugeot.

Thank you to the wonderful team at the University of Pittsburgh Press, in particular Maria Sticco and Alex Wolfe, who I worked closely with. To my editor, mentor, and dear friend Ed Ochester, you allowed this to be possible. I am forever indebted.

Yusef Komunyakaa, Naomi Shihab Nye, and Tony Barnstone, I can't thank you enough for your continued words and guidance.

Subhi Hadidi, it will never be enough—*shukran kteer*. Alberto López, I would not have found the spin of Andalucía without you. David Groff, your advice and editorship were indispensable—I am profoundly thankful that I continue journeying with you. To Michael, there are no sufficient words.

To all those who travel with me in one form or another, thank you. Finally, to my family and friends, you are forever luminous around me.